BRITAIN

A PICTURE BOOK TO REMEMBER HER BY

This royal throne of Kings, this scepter'd isle,
This earth of majesty, this seat of Mars,
This other Eden, demi-paradise,
This fortress built by Nature for herself,
Against infection and the hand of war,
This happy breed of men, this little world,
This precious stone set in the silver sea,
Which serves it in the office of a wall,
Or as a moat defensive to a house,
Against the envy of less happier lands,
This blessed plot, this earth, this realm, this England,

"Richard II" Act 2 Sc. 1 32 48
–Shakespeare–
A.D. 1564 – 1616

PUBLISHED BY COLOUR LIBRARY INTERNATIONAL LTD.,
80/82. COOMBE ROAD.
NEW MALDEN. SURREY.   TEL. 01-942-7781

PRODUCED BY TED SMART, C.L.I.
1.st EDITION 1975.
2.nd EDITION 1976.
© COLOUR LIBRARY INTERNATIONAL LTD.

Printed by OFSA Milano and bound by L.E.G.O. Vicenza Italy

ISBN 0 904681 04 1

COLOUR LIBRARY INTERNATIONAL

SCOTLAND

Isle of Man

WALES

ISLES OF
SCILLY
St Marys

Berwick upon Tweed

Alnwick

Whitley Bay
Newcastle
Tynemouth
South Shields

Carlisle
Hexham
Northumbria
Alston
Durham

Maryport
Cockermouth
Penrith
Barnard Castle
Redcar
Saltburn by the Sea

Keswick
Appleby
Darlington
Whitby

Whitehaven
English Lake
County
Grasmere
Ambleside
Windermere
Kendal
Richmond
Helmsley
Scarborough
Filey

Millom
Grange over Sands
Ripon
Yorkshire

Ulverston
Bridlington

Morecambe & Heysham
Lancaster
Harrogate
York
Beverley
Hornsea

Fleetwood
Skipton
Burnsall
Hull
Withernsea

Thornton Cleveleys
Keighley
Ilkley
Leeds

Blackpool
Preston
Bradford
Scunthorpe

Lytham St Annes
Blackburn
Grimsby
Cleethorpes

Southport
Bolton
Glossop
Sheffield
English
Shires

Wallasey
Manchester
Liverpool
The West
Chesterfield
Lincoln
Mablethorpe
Sutton-on-Sea

Birkenhead
Buxton
Bakewell
Woodhall Spa
Skegness

Chester
Matlock
Newark on Trent
Boston

Derby
Ilkeston
Nottingham
Spalding
Sheringham
Cromer

Oswestry
Shrewsbury
Stafford
Ashby-de-la-Zouch
Wells next
the Sea

Much Wenlock
Lichfield
Leicester
Kings Lynn
Great Yarmouth
Norwich

Wolverhampton
Nuneaton
Wisbech
Lowestoft

Bridgnorth
Birmingham
Coventry
Peterborough
East Anglia

Ludlow
Droitwich
Kenilworth
Royal Leamington Spa
Rugby
Ely
Southwold

Leominster
Redditch
Warwick
Northampton
Bury St Edmunds
Aldeburgh

Heart of
England
Worcester
Stratford upon Avon
Cambridge
Ipswich

Malvern
Upton upon Severn
Bedford
Saffron Walden
Felixstowe

Hereford
Banbury
Braintree
Colchester
Harwich

Ross on Wye
Tewkesbury
Luton
Welwyn Garden City
Frinton-on-Sea
Clacton-on-Sea

Cheltenham
Aylesbury
The Thames
and
Chilterns
Oxford
St Albans

Gloucester
Cirencester
Abingdon
Southend

Stroud
Malmesbury
High Wycombe
Isle of Sheppey
Whitstable
Herne Bay
Margate

Swindon
Maidenhead
Greater
London
Rochester
Broadstairs
Ramsgate

Bristol
Clevedon
Bath
Marlborough
Windsor
Faversham
Sandwich

Combe Martin
Minehead
Porlock
Weston
super Mare
Burnham on Sea
Devizes
Bradford on Avon
Newbury
Reading
Egham
Maidstone
Canterbury
Dover

Lynton
Wells
Frome
Warminster
Wilton
Winchester
Guildford
Dorking
Royal Tunbridge Wells
Folkestone
Hythe

Ilfracombe
Woolacombe
Westward Ho!
Watchet
Williton
Bridgwater
Shepton Mallet
Langport
Salisbury
Haslemere
South East England
Rye
Hastings

Barnstaple
Dulverton
Taunton
Wellington
Yeovil
Romsey
Southampton
Chichester
Lewes
Bexhill on Sea

Bideford
South Molton
Ilminster
Sherborne
Bognor Regis
Worthing
Brighton
Newhaven
Seaford
Eastbourne

Bude
Great Torrington
Tiverton
Chard
Portsmouth
Littlehampton

The West Country
Okehampton
Honiton
Bridport
Dorchester
Poole
Christchurch
Bournemouth
Cowes
Newport
Ryde

Tintagel
Exeter
Ottery St Mary
Lyme Regis
Weymouth
Swanage
Sandown
Shanklin
Ventnor

Camelford
Launceston
Bovey Tracey
Seaton
Sidmouth

Padstow
Polzeath
Tavistock
Newton
Abbot
Budleigh Salterton
Exmouth

Newquay
Ashburton
Buckfastleigh
Dawlish
Teignmouth
Torbay

St Austell
Bodmin
Totnes

Truro
Camborne
Looe
Plymouth
Dartmouth

St Ives
Helston
Fowey
Salcombe
Kingsbridge

Penzance
Falmouth

Lands End

Festival Hall and River Thames, London *(Above)*
On the banks of the wonderful 'Old Father Thames', the Festival
Hall was originally built in 1951 for the Festival of Britain. It
comprises several concert halls and smaller rooms for intimate
recitals. It has been expanded as part of the South Bank Development which includes the National Film Theatre. The modern
aspect of creamy white stone blends well with the traditional
London.

The Life Guards *(Opposite)*

The Houses of Parliament and Big Ben, London

London by Night *(Bottom Right)*
The famous dome of St. Paul's Cathedral is floodlit in the night sky and stands out clearly as a masterpiece of the architect, Sir Christopher Wren. In the foreground is H.M.S. Discovery, the ship that Scott used for polar research and which is now a Royal Navy and Royal Marines recruiting vessel.

The Choir Stalls of Westminster Abbey (Above)
The Collegiate Church of St. Peter in Westminster, under its less formal title of Westminster Abbey, holds within its walls a wealth of history. When entering the Cathedral one cannot help pausing and gazing in awe at the richness of this building. The view here is of the choir stalls looking towards the highly-decorated organ loft and stained-glass windows of the West Entrance.

St. Paul's Cathedral, London *(Below)*

Designed by Sir Christopher Wren and built between 1675 and 1710 of Portland Stone at a cost of £1,000,000 — a considerable sum at that time — St. Paul's is the burial place of many famous men — Nelson, the Duke of Wellington and the painter, Turner to name but a few. In 1965 the State Funeral of Sir Winston Churchill was held here. The height of the building, including the cross, is 365 ft.

Tower of London *(Overleaf)*

The Tower as it now stands was built by William the Conqueror about 1078, and added to at various times later. It served as a fortress, Palace and prison, and has many tragic associations. The White Tower houses a splendid collection of armour. The Crown Jewels are housed in the Wakefield Tower.

Clovelly, North Devon *(Below and opposite)*
Clovelly described by Charles Kingsley as ''a straggling village
of irregularly-shaped lichen-covered cottages on so steep an
incline that the base of the one is on a level with the roof of its
neighbour''. The single street of steps descends 400 feet to the
pebbled beach and a tiny quay, no wheeled traffic is permitted,
cars being parked above the village.

Brixham, Devon *(Top Left)*
A fishing harbour, Brixham is a popular resort for holiday makers who watch the fishing boats or walk along the narrow streets. On the quay there is a statue to commemorate William of Orange's landing in 1688 and a milestone marking the end of a former turnpike.

Polperro, Cornwall *(Below)*
Situated in a sheltered inlet between two headlands, Polperro is one of the most popular villages in Cornwall. Backed by a steep hill, the harbour is a most attractive feature and provides a haven for many colourful fishing vessels. It is overlooked by typical Cornish stone-built houses, the quaint old 'House on Props' being of particular interest.

Oddicombe Beach, Babbacombe, near Torquay, Devonshire *(Opposite Bottom Left)*
The busy and ever-popular resort of Torquay has many pretty suburbs, not the least of which is Oddicombe. The sands, sailing and cliff-top walks in this area are superb and Babbacombe Downs give excellent views of the coast line. For the convenience of summer visitors a cliff railway descends to Oddicombe and Babbacombe beaches.

Land's End, Cornwall *(Opposite Bottom Right)*
The surf thunders against the granite cliffs on the extreme south-westerly tip of England looking out to the Longships Lighthouse. Beyond, on a clear day, the Isles of Scilly can be seen and the coast is noted for its rugged beauty. By road, "John O'Groats" is just 873 miles away.

Corfe Castle, Dorset *(Left)*
Set in the lovely Purbeck Hills, this impressive ruined castle dominates the village of Corfe Castle. Dating from Norman times, it was the object of a famous siege during the Civil War. In 1646 it was reduced to its present condition by gunpowder. Many attractive and interesting old houses are to be found in the village itself.

Cockington Forge, Torquay, Devonshire *(Right)*
Cockington, a quaint little village about half a mile west of Torquay, attracts many visitors. It is famous for its thatched cottages and, of course, the old forge which is still in working order. Visitors may take a ride round the village in a gaily painted horse-drawn trap.

Plymouth, Devon *(Bottom Right)*
Plymouth, port and naval base, is, of course, most famous for its associations with Sir Francis Drake. Here on Plymouth Hoe he played bowls as the Spanish Armada drew nearer. It was from here too that the Pilgrim Fathers sailed in the Mayflower to America. Much of the town has been rebuilt since the war, as can be seen from the modern shopping centre above.

The Old Boathouse, Bantham, Devon *(Below)*
Bantham is one of many pretty villages on the inlets and creeks of the Devon coast. On the mouth of the Devon Avon, Bantham offers splendid cliff scenery for ramblers and sandy floors appear in the coves at low tide for sunbathers, but most places like this boathouse are best explored by boat.

Roman Baths, Bath, Somerset *(Right)*

At one time a city of high fashion visited by the aristocracy to "take the waters", Bath Spa is famous for its finely preserved Roman remains. The baths are fed by the only natural hot springs in Britain and, in the Pump Room, the waters, believed to be particularly beneficial, can still be tasted. The central tower of the Abbey Church can be seen in the background.

The Winter Gardens, Weston-super-Mare, Somerset *(Top Left)*

On a sheltered bay in the Bristol Channel, Weston-super-Mare is a favourite seaside resort with good bathing, cinemas and theatres. The attractive Italian Winter Gardens with flowers in bloom all the year round are popular with summer and winter visitors.

Clifton Suspension Bridge, Bristol *(Bottom Left)*

The Clifton Suspension Bridge, designed by Brunel, spans the Avon Gorge some 245 ft. above the river. Beneath the Observatory on Clifton Down where a camera obscura is situated, is the entrance to the Giant's Cave. A passage leads downwards to a large cave in the side of the Gorge, an impressive viewpoint.

Pulteney Bridge, Bath, Somerset *(Below)*

Delightfully situated on the winding Somerset Avon, Bath was built by the Romans who made elaborate uses of the only natural hot springs in Britain. Pulteney Bridge, designed by Robert Adam, is flanked with shops and adds to the charm of a town that has always been noted for its elegance.

Chipping Campden, Gloucestershire *(Above)*

The mellow stone of the Cotswolds is enhanced by this display of spring blossom in the beautiful unspoiled country town of Chipping Campden. Once the capital of the Cotswold wool trade, the industry thrived here and from the proceeds many impressive manor houses were built. The Fifteenth Century 'wool' church has several fine old brasses and magnificent frontals—believed to be the oldest in the country.

Salisbury Cathedral, Wiltshire *(Top Right)*

The spire of Salisbury Cathedral, the highest in England, rises from the "water meadows" of the Avon with undiminishing impact from different view points. Begun in 1220, the cathedral has a dial-less clock dating from 1326 and the cathedral library contains one of the four copies of the Magna Carta.

The Severn Bridge, Gloucestershire *(Left)*

The elegant and magnificent Severn Bridge, Linking Aust and Beachley in Gloucestershire, also crosses the River Wye into Monmouth. It was opened in September 1966, several months ahead of schedule, and replaces the Aust car ferry which had carried many thousands of passengers during its 35 years of operation. One of the longest bridges in Europe with a central span of 3,240 ft. and side spans each of 1,000 ft., the road is carried some 120 ft. above high water.

Stonehenge, Wiltshire *(Bottom Right)*

These famous and fascinating prehistoric stone circles, of unknown origin and purpose, stand near the A344 — just west of Amesbury. Believed to have been brought from Pembrokeshire, Wales, the stones average a height of $13\frac{1}{2}$ ft. above ground and $4\frac{1}{2}$ ft. below, each stone being approximately 26 tons in weight. The whole site is surrounded by earthworks some 300 ft. in diameter.

The Seven Stars, Fullerton, Hampshire *(Top Right)*

What better way to idle away a summer's afternoon than watching a river from a quiet nook in the sun? Here at Fullerton, The Seven Stars provides a seat and refreshments while the weirs keep the clear waters of the River Test to a musical pace in the midst of the beautiful Hampshire countryside.

Swan Green, near Lyndhurst, Hampshire *(Left)*

Swan Green is the perfect setting for a friendly game of cricket. Situated near Lyndhurst it is an ideal starting point for trips into the attractive woodland of the New Forest. There are plenty of interesting trees and shrubs to see and a visit is made more enjoyable by the ever curious New Forest ponies.

Godshill, Isle of Wight *(Bottom Right)*

Godshill, a picturesque little village in the south of the Island, not far from Shanklin, is famous for its quaint old thatched cottages. In the village stands the 14th Century church with its square stone tower and old clock, noted for its chancel graves.

Southampton, Hampshire *(Below)*

Famous port from which the great liners set out across the Atlantic, Southampton has its origins deep in history. It was from the West Quay in 1620 that the Pilgrim Fathers set sail on the first lap of their long journey. From here too, in 1414, King Henry V and his army left for France on their way to Victory at the Battle of Agincourt.

Glyndebourne, Sussex *(Below)*
Concert goers picnic in the garden during intermission in style and formal attire.

Eastbourne, Sussex *(Top Right)*
A charming resort on the south coast, Eastbourne nestles beneath the South Downs. To the west the towering chalk cliffs of Beachy Head rise to a height of 575 ft. The town it self is pleasantly laid out with a wide promenade and beautiful gardens, a blaze of colour during the summer months.

The Royal Pavilion, Brighton, Sussex *(Bottom Right)*
The Royal Pavilion, begun in 1784, was rebuilt after 1817 in an Oriental style for the Prince of Wales (later George IV) who frequently resided here. Nearby are the ever-popular 'Lanes'. This is a small precinct of narrow alleys housing antique and bric-a-brac shops as well as modern boutiques.

Scotney Castle, near Lamberhurst, Kent *(Below)*
On an island in the middle of a lake, what could be more romantic
than Scotney Castle? Though mostly ruined, it is all the more
picturesque. The village of Lamberhurst is delightful with its old
houses and not far off are the 13th century remains of Bayham
Abbey. The adjacent mansion is the seat of the Marquess of
Camden.

Canterbury Cathedral, Kent *(Above)*
The cathedral and rooftops of Canterbury seem to reflect the timeless legends of the Black Prince's exploits, the tragedy of Thomas á Becket and the Roman occupation of Durovernum. By way of contrast, part of industrial history is also preserved here in the form of the charming engine "Invicta", one of the earliest locomotives.

Windsor Castle, Berkshire *(Below and Bottom Right)*
One of the first thrills for the visitor to England is a view of Windsor Castle. Not far from London, it is within easy reach for the tourist — and for the Royal Family whose standard is eagerly watched for. Originally built by William the Conqueror the castle is delightfully situated on the Thames and surrounded by beautiful parks.

St. George's Chapel, Windsor Castle *(Right)*
St. George's Chapel was commenced at the end of the Fifteenth Century by Edward IV as a chapel of the Order of the Garter. Its fine Perpendicular fan vaulting, completed in 1528, is of special note. On either side of the choir hang the insignia, swords, helmets and banners of the Knights of the Garter. It is the burial place of many kings, among them Edward IV, Henry VIII, his third bride Jane Seymour, and Charles I.

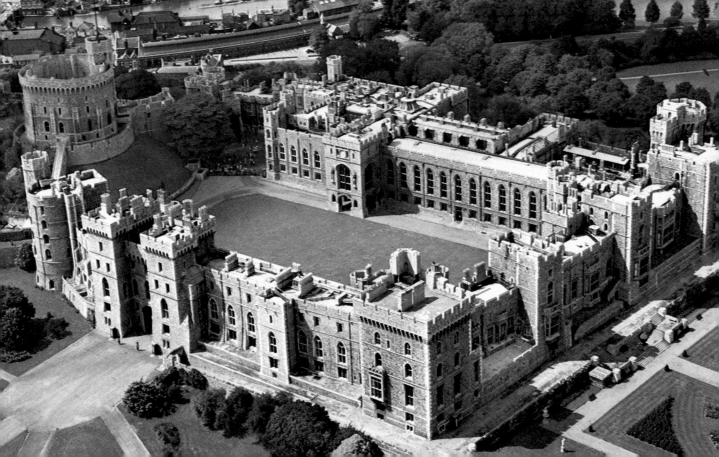

Polesden Lacey Estate, near Great Bookham, Surrey *(Above)*
The great beech trees of the woodlands around Polesden Lacey House make russet carpets for the feet of the rambler. King George VI and Queen Elizabeth, when Duke and Duchess of York, spent their honeymoon in this idyllic spot in 1923. The house itself, bequeathed to the National Trust by the Hon. Mrs. Ronald Greville, a noted Edwardian hostess, has a fine collection of paintings, porcelain and furniture.

Kingston-upon-Thames, Surrey *(Bottom Right)*
Kingston-upon-Thames maintains a bustling individuality amid the commuter suburbs of Greater London. Near the main market, seen here, there is an apple market and a Monday cattle market. A royal land, even before the Saxon kings were consecrated here at the coronation stone, Kingston has always been a communal spot on the River Thames as proved by archaeological finds preserved in the museum.

Goring Lock, Oxfordshire *(Top Right)*

The picturesque little village of Goring lies on the River Thames not far north of Pangbourne in a vale of the Chilterns where the Icknield Way bridged the River on its long journey from East Anglia to the South West. In the belfry of the church, built in Norman style, is an ancient bell, cast in 1290.

Magdalen Tower and the Punters' Station, Oxford
(Below)

The old university town of Oxford is still dominated by the buildings and traditions that date from medieval times. On May morning a 17th century hymn is sung at the top of Magdalen Tower at sunrise and this is later followed by a free-for-all on the punts with much splashing and pushing-in.

Henley-on-Thames, Oxfordshire *(Bottom Right)*

A well-known town on the River Thames, Henley is, of course, most famous for its Regatta, held each year during the first week of July. Much of the architecture in the town is Georgian and some of it earlier. The Church is in the Gothic style with many interesting old stones.

Royal Shakespeare Theatre, Stratford-upon-Avon, Warwickshire *(Top Right)*

Beautifully situated on the River Avon, the Memorial Theatre, designed by Elizabeth Scott, was opened in 1932 and replaces the original theatre burned down in 1925. Festival performances of Shakespeare's plays are given here from April to October. The memorial also contains a library, picture gallery and museum. The town of Stratford is renowned, of course, as the birthplace of Shakespeare in 1564.

Welford-on-Avon, Warwickshire *(Below)*

The thatched and timbered cottages of Welford-on-Avon nestle among the flowers as if big cities had never been heard of. The village maypole with its unsophisticated stripes and the old lychgate by the churchyard complete the aura of rural tranquility and friendliness that appeals to even the most business-like heart.

Anne Hathaway's Cottage, Shottery, Warwickshire *(Bottom Right)*

By taking the picturesque footpath across the fields from Stratford, one reaches the pretty village of Shottery. It was here in this charming half-timbered Elizabethan farmhouse that Anne Hathaway was born. Many interesting relics and original Hathaway furniture can be seen in the cottage.

The Botanical Gardens, Birmingham *(Below)*
An unexpected glimpse of the industrial and University city of Birmingham showing the Botanical Gardens which lie hard by the famous cricket ground at Edgbaston. The town itself has many interesting old buildings, among them the restored Church of St. Martin where members of the De Bermingham family are buried.

Lady Godiva Statue, Coventry *(Above)*
Famed in recent years for the wonderful new cathedral designed by Sir Basil Spence and opened by Her Majesty the Queen in 1962, Coventry has many historic associations. One of the most famous is the old tale of Lady Godiva, whose statue is pictured here. The unfortunate 'Peeping Tom' is also commemorated by an effigy overlooking Hertford Street.

The Bull Ring, Birmingham, Warwickshire *(Above)*
The recently developed Bull Ring site with its modern skyscrapers and bright neon signs contrasts vividly with the older areas of this University city. Of interest are the 17th Century Stratford House, recently restored and Aston House, completed in 1635, which is now a museum.

Houghton Mill, Huntingdonshire *(Right)*
Attractively situated on the River Ouse and a popular boating centre, the pretty old village of Houghton is noted for its water mill pictured here. The mill, property of the National Trust, has been immaculately preserved and is now leased to the Youth Hostels Association.

The Backs, Cambridge *(Top Left)*
These beautiful lawns and gardens, much frequented by students and open to the public during daylight hours, sweep down to the famous River Cam which is spanned by several magnificent bridges.

King's College, Cambridge *(Bottom Left)*
The city of Cambridge is of course famed for its University, founded in the thirteenth century, with Peterhouse the oldest college. King's College was founded by King Henry VI, in 1441-3. The building of the superb Chapel was commenced in 1446, and took nearly a century to complete. The stained glass windows are particularly outstanding in their beauty.

Duxford Mill, Cambridgeshire *(Below)*
Well-kept Duxford Mill with its beautiful surroundings is one of many mills sprinkled liberally on the rich flat lands of Cambridgeshire. They once provided a source of energy for this thriving agricultural region before steam and electricity were mastered. Though most of them are no longer used for their original function they are popular as residences.

Epping Forest, Essex *(Top Left)*
Epping Forest, with its 5,600 acres of beautiful, woodland scenery, is a quiet haven not twenty miles from the great metropolis of London. The Forest has belonged to the City of London since 1863. South of the town of Epping stands Waltham Abbey, dating from 1556, where King Harold, killed at the Battle of Hastings, is buried.

Finchingfield, Essex *(Below)*
One of the prettiest villages in Essex, not far from Thaxted, Finchingfield has many interesting houses and cottages. The church is also of note, being Norman in origin, of which the tower still remains. An old post-mill still stands in the village.

River Blackwater, near Stisted, Essex *(Bottom Left)*
The pretty river Blackwater rises near the village of Seward's End and then meanders through the Essex countryside to Maldon, where it opens out into a wide estuary. On its journey, it passes the silk-manufacturing town of Braintree and the lace-making village of Coggeshall.

Willy Lott's Cottage, Flatford Mill, Suffolk *(Below)*
Willy Lott's Cottage is best known for its appearance in John Constable's famous painting . . . The Hay Wain. Flatford Mill lies near the estuary of the River Stour and it is in this area that one can find many of the typically English landscapes favoured by the artist.

(Opposite) a master craftsman at work thatching the roof of a house in Suffolk.

Tombland Alley, Norwich, Norfolk *(Below)*

Norwich is a city of great history. Once a centre of the wool trade, it has many venerable houses and over thirty old Parish Churches. It was the home of the ''Norwich School'' of artists and Lord Nelson went to the Grammar School just off this quiet corner at Tombland Alley.

The Norfolk Broads, Norfolk *(Top Right)*

Bounded by the towns of Lowestoft, Sea Palling and Norwich, the area known as the Broads is traversed by over 200 miles of inland waterways. The beautiful, green countryside is very low and flat and the stately windmills are a familiar feature. It is a popular holiday centre for boating enthusiasts from all over Britain.

Horning Ferry, Norfolk *(Opposite)*

Horning lies on the River Bure and is a popular Broads holiday centre. The picturesque little 'pub' in the picture is one of many offering their hospitality to the growing numbers of holiday-makers who travel the charming rivers and broads each summer in brightly painted boats.

The Tulip Fields, Spalding, Lincolnshire *(Top Right)*

Spalding lies in the heart of the Fen District, an area formed by the gradual silting up of a large bay. The fertile soil is ideal for bulbs, and the town of Spalding is the centre of the English bulb industry. From April to May, the fields are a blaze of colour when the daffodils and tulips are in bloom.

Matlock Bath, Derbyshire *(Left)*

Matlock Bath stands on the banks of the River Derwent at the foot of the magnificent Derbyshire Peaks. A spa town, it has medicinal springs and baths. To the north is Matlock, at the foot of the picturesque Darley Dale. Dominated by the towering Heights of Abraham, this is an ideal centre for touring the Peaks and Dales.

Lincoln Cathedral *(Bottom Right)*

The magnificent cathedral dates from the Eleventh Century. Its three elegant towers are of particular interest. In the magnificent Central Tower hangs 'Great Tom of Lincoln', a bell weighing $5\frac{1}{2}$ tons. The best of the four copies of the Magna Carta is found here and the building contains many fine examples of wood carving. Within the beautiful Angel Choir the famous 'Lincoln Imp' can be seen.

Trent Building, University of Nottingham *(Below)*

Founded in 1881, the University College moved from its original site to the Trent Building, University Park, in 1928. The park and the building were the gift of Sir Jesse Boot, the first Lord Trent. The University was granted its Charter in 1948 and now has over 5,000 full-time students. The latest development is a Medical School and Teaching Hospital on an adjacent site.

Muker, Yorkshire *(Top Left)*
Near the beautiful waterfall of Kisdon Force in the romantic Yorkshire Dales stands the picturesque village of Muker. In crossing the Dales the scenery changes from wild and lonely moors to the waterfalls of Wensleydale, the notable How Stean Gorge, near Lofthouse, and the potholes and caves of Ingleton.

Scarborough, Yorkshire *(Top Right)*
From the harbour the fishing boats put out to catch fish in the North Sea. The town is a popular holiday resort with a sandy bay to the north and south. The 12th Century "Three Mariners", originally a hostelry, is now an interesting museum and several other buildings in the town are of historic interest.

Robin Hood's Bay, Yorkshire *(Bottom Right)*
Robin Hood's Bay, a small fishing village a few miles south-east of Whitby, is dominated to the landward by the high Fylingdales Moor. The Bay, sandy at low tide, is backed by tall cliffs and affords excellent bathing. The magnificent cliff scenery is impressive, particularly to the south at Ravenscar, another small clifftop village with a little rocky beach.

Queen's Gardens, Hull *(Below)*
Famous port with extensive docks, Kingston-upon-Hull, as the town is officially known, is a centre of the fishing industry in Great Britain. It stands at the confluence of the Hull River with the great Humber and has associations with William Wilberforce, born here in 1759. A tall column bearing his statue overlooks the Queen's Gardens.

Bolton Abbey, Wharfedale, Yorkshire *(Top Right)*

Bolton Abbey stands on the River Wharfe some seven miles north east of Skipton. Dating from the 13th Century and now in ruins, the old nave forms part of the present Parish Church. The beautiful Wharfedale in the West Riding is part of the Yorkshire Dales National Park.

Fountains Abbey, Yorkshire *(Below)*

This great Cistercian Abbey was founded in the 12th century by Archbishop Thurston with twelve monks and it took three centuries to complete. Still well-preserved, it stands on the River Skell within Studley Park where a Norway spruce has grown to 156 feet. Nearby the church and house of Studley Royal and the beautiful Fountains Hall are well worth a visit.

Aysgarth Falls, Wensleydale, Yorkshire *(Bottom Right)*

Aysgarth Falls form part of the picturesque and tortuous River Ure as it winds its way down to join the Ouse. It flows through the pastoral beauty of Wensleydale, one of the less rugged dales of Yorkshire, especially famous for its excellent cheese.

Little Moreton Hall, Cheshire *(Below)*
Swans glide idly on the moat of the beautiful black and white gabled house that is Little Moreton Hall. Built between 1559 and 1590 with its carved corner posts and ornate windows it has scarcely been changed since then. The Gallery, with its original panelling, the heraldically-carved fireplaces and the great hall are all worthy of a visit.

Chester Cathedral (Above)

Chester, the former Roman city of Deva, is of great historical interest. Much of the city walls remain, as do the attractive 'Rows' – old first floor shopping arcades. The beautiful cathedral pictured here is mainly Fourteenth Century and was once a Benedictine Abbey. It contains many fine examples of richly carved woodwork.

Chester, Cheshire (Right)

The picturesque 'rows', with their shops raised above the street level, are unique. Some preserve fine crypts or cellars. There are many lovely old half-timbered houses, including 'God's Providence House', 'Bishop Lloyd's Palace', 'Leche House', and the 'Stanley Palace'. The 'Falcon', the 'King Edgar', and the 'Bear and Billet' are fine timbered Inns.

The Metropolitan Cathedral of Christ the King, Liverpool, Lancashire (Below)

The new Metropolitan Cathedral is a true wonder of modern architecture. Designed by Sir Frederick Gibberd, the outer wall is formed by sixteen small buildings, eight of which are chapels, separated by sheets of deep blue glass. The magnificent structure is crowned by a circle of stained glass windows so vast that a whole new technique in working the glass had to be developed.

Liverpool Docks, Lancashire (Top Right)

Liverpool is important for its university, fine cathedrals and art galleries, but most of all it is a port on the Mersey estuary with docks that extend for seven miles. The Royal Liver building in the distance looks on as the tugs manoeuvre the cargo ships that ply all over the world.

Liverpool Docks (Opposite)

This setting of Liverpool Docks belies its importance as a busy and essential link in the importing and exporting of goods. Situated on the Mersey estuary, the dockside frontage extends for seven miles. The University city has many interesting buildings as well as some fine Georgian houses, particularly in Rodney Street where Gladstone was born.

Blackpool, Lancashire *(Right and Below)*
One of the most popular holiday resorts in England, Blackpool has a rich variety of all-weather entertainments to offer the visitor. The Tower, the piers, the Pleasure Beach with its carnival atmosphere, golden sands . . . not forgetting the spectacular illuminations, all contribute to the happiness that Blackpool is noted for.

Derwent Water, Cumberland *(Top Right)*

One of the largest stretches of water in the Lake District, the lovely Derwent Water presents its early morning face reflecting the cool mauve of the heather-covered mountains. Coleridge and Shelley stayed at Keswick on the northern extremity of the lake and there are many fine viewpoints.

Lingmoor Fell and the Langdale Pikes, Westmorland
(Left)

Above the village of Langdale rise the famous, lofty Langdale Pikes and below lies the wild and desolate Stickle Tarn. The beautiful Lake District, well-known for climbing and magnificent scenery, stretches away on all sides — rolling hills and mountains interspersed with lakes and tarns.

Tarn Hows, near Coniston, Lake District, Lancashire
(Bottom Right)

Winter brings new contrasts and textures to the green mountains and blue waters of this delightful tarn, or small lake. Tarn Hows is a part of the wonderful Lake District where many writers found inspiration or relaxation; nearby Coniston is the birthplace of the writer and critic Ruskin and Lord Tennyson had a residence there

Wast Water, Wasdale, Cumberland *(Below)*

Beneath the peaks of Sca Fell and Great Gable the wild, lonely Wast Water lies in a deep valley. Fed by tributaries from the Black Sail and Sty Head Passes, the lake is drained from its southern extremity by the River Irt which joins the sea at Ravenglass. To the north is Wasdale Head, a popular climbing centre.

The Cathedral, Durham (Below)

One of the finest Norman buildings in England, Durham Cathedral stands above the River Wear on which the town is built. The tomb of the Venerable Bede is to be found here and on the north door is a 'sanctuary knocker' believed to have secured asylum for several hundred people during the Fifteenth and early Sixteenth Centuries. Parts of the Monastery buildings still remain.

Newcastle-upon-Tyne (Top Right)

Well-known port and industrial city, noted for the manufacture of armaments, ships and famous too for its coal, Newcastle was once the point where the Tyne was bridged by the Romans, known as Pons Aelii. Three magnificent bridges still span the River here, one dating from 1849.

New Civic Centre, Newcastle-upon-Tyne (Opposite)

Old and new stand side by side in this historic city on the famous River Tyne. There are many fine buildings of historic interest, notably the castle, the Thirteenth Century Black Gate and the Roman remains to be found in the University Quadrangle. Our picture shows the modern Civic Centre, completed in November, 1968 and opened by the King of Norway.

Lindisfarne Castle, Holy Island, Northumberland
(Below)

Lindisfarne or Holy Island can be reached, except at high tide, by crossing the sands on foot. Designated an area of outstanding natural beauty, the Island's old buildings are of great interest, notably the 16th Century Castle, recently restored. The Abbey, now in ruins, is of Norman origin and the Parish Church is also very old, dating from the 12th Century.

Dunstankburgh Castle, near Craster, Northumberland *(Above)*

Perched on the Northumberland coast, Dunstanburgh Castle presides over a stretch of sea and coast that has been officially declared an Area of Outstanding Natural Beauty. The ruins of this 16th century castle bear witness to the fortunes of war . . . it changed hands five times during the Wars of the Roses.

SCOTLAND

Edinburgh Castle

Abbotsford House, Roxburghshire *(Above)*
Dating from 1817, Abbotsford House, the last home of Sir Walter Scott who died here in 1832, stands on the banks of the lovely River Tweed. Surrounded by magnificent woods, Abbotsford holds many relics of the author, and the study in particular, has been preserved as he left it. To the south-east rise the beautiful Eildon Hills, affording wonderful views of the Scott Country.

Culzean Castle, Ayrshire *(Top Left)*
A splendid edifice, the castle dates from 1777 and holds a commanding position overlooking the sweep of Culzean Bay. A stronghold of the Kennedys for many years, the building contains many interesting relics of the family. A flat in the castle was presented to General Eisenhower as a Scottish residence during his lifetime. The grounds are of particular beauty and are open to visitors during the summer months.

Blair Castle, Blair Atholl, Perthshire *(Bottom Left)*
Set in its own wooded grounds, Blair Castle is the seat of the Duke of Atholl and is open to the public. It is unique in being the headquarters of the only private army in the realm — the Duke's own bodyguard received its colours from Queen Victoria in 1845. The nearby village of Blair Atholl is an excellent centre for exploring the many glens that meet here.

Inverary Castle, Argyllshire *(Right)*
One of the best known castles in Scotland, Inverary — for long the hereditary seat of the Dukes of Argyll — is situated on the bank of the river Aray. The present castle dates from 1745 and is seen at its best in sunshine immediately after a shower of rain when it appears to change colour.

Dunure Castle, Ayrshire *(Below)*
This beautiful sunset at Dunure shows the fragmentary remains of the castle on the cliffs in silhouette and gives no hint of a cruel Earl of Cassillis who is said to have roasted Allan Stewart, commendator of Crossraguel Abbey, over a slow fire until the victim consented to surrender the abbey lands. Dunure is a popular seaside resort and fishing village.

Melrose Abbey, Roxburghshire *(Above)*
Beautiful Melrose Abbey is one of the prime attractions of the
border county of Roxburgh. Founded in 1136 by David I, the
abbey suffered from many later invasions and was used as a
quarry after the Reformation. Gifted to the nation in 1918 by
the Duke of Buccleuch, it has many associations with Scottish
Royalty and the heart of Robert the Bruce is buried beneath the
High Altar.

George Square, Glasgow, Lanarkshire (Below)
The elaborate granite building of the City Chambers looks out onto George Square, the Cenotaph designed by Sir John Burnet and the 80 ft. high monument bearing a statue of Sir Walter Scott. The attractive gardens, ablaze with flowers, are a haven for the people of this busy city.

Sunset on the Clyde, Glasgow (Top Right)
The magnificent River Clyde with its immense docks and extensive shipbuilding industry is world famous. The city of Glasgow has grown and expanded over the past 150 years, and is Scotland's largest city and seaport. Silhouetted against the sunset, the cranes and masts of Clydeside reach up to the sky while the smooth glittering river flows gently down past Greenock and Dunoon, to the Firth of Clyde and the Atlantic Ocean.

University and Art Gallery, Glasgow (Bottom Right)
Glasgow University, founded in 1450, is particularly noted for its library containing many rare books. Nearby the Museum and Art Gallery, opened in 1901, house the famous Burrell Collection, together with one of the most comprehensive collections of paintings in Britain, representing Scottish, Dutch and French artists.

Firth of Clyde from Lyle Hill, Greenock, Renfrewshire *(Below)*

Lyle Hill, Greenock, affords a magnificent view of the Firth of Clyde, always busy with shipping. The famous Cross of Lorraine was erected on Lyle Hill, in memory of the Free French sailors who gave their lives in the Battle of the Atlantic during the second World War.

Queen Elizabeth II Passing Cloch Point, Renfrewshire *(Top Right)*

Cloch Point overlooks the Clyde Estuary opposite the popular resort and yachting centre of Dunoon. The famous Cloch Point Lighthouse, built in 1797, is a well-known landmark. The graceful liner, Queen Elizabeth II, built on Clydeside, was launched in September, 1967.

Cardwell Bay and Gourock, Renfrewshire *(Bottom Right)*

Gourock lies on a sheltered bay on the Firth of Clyde and is a popular holiday and yachting resort. Across the Firth lie Holy Loch and Loch Long, with their magnificent surrounding scenery. On the summit of Lyle Hill, from which this view is taken, stands the Cross of Lorraine, erected in memory of those Free French who died in the Battle of the Atlantic.

Ross Fountain and The Castle, Edinburgh *(Below)*
The origins of Edinburgh Castle are lost in history. An impressive fortress, it overlooks Princes Street and the attractive Old Town. It has changed hands many times in the course of the years and is the scene of many historic events. The famous Prince Charles Edward — 'Bonnie Prince Charlie' — although holding the town, did not succeed in capturing the Castle. In the foreground, stands the ornate Ross Fountain, built in Paris for the Paris Exhibition by Daniel Ross, a gun maker, and gifted by him to Edinburgh in 1869.

Princes Street, Edinburgh *(Top Right)*
The busy thoroughfare of Princes Street runs through the heart of this historic city, the capital of Scotland. Dominating the scene is the famous castle, its origins lost in legendary time. From the castle, the High Street or Royal Mile leads to the Palace of Holyroodhouse and Holyrood Park which includes Arthur's Seat, a rugged extinct volcano commanding fine views of the city and its extensive docks on the Firth of Forth.

Edinburgh by Night, Midlothian *(Bottom Right)*
The National Monument and Nelson Monument stand on Calton Hill from whence we look down over the lighted streets of the town. In the background is the Castle, steeped in history and originally known as ''Duneadain'' or the ''fort on a hill''. To the left is the spire of the ancient Greyfriars Church, built in 1612.

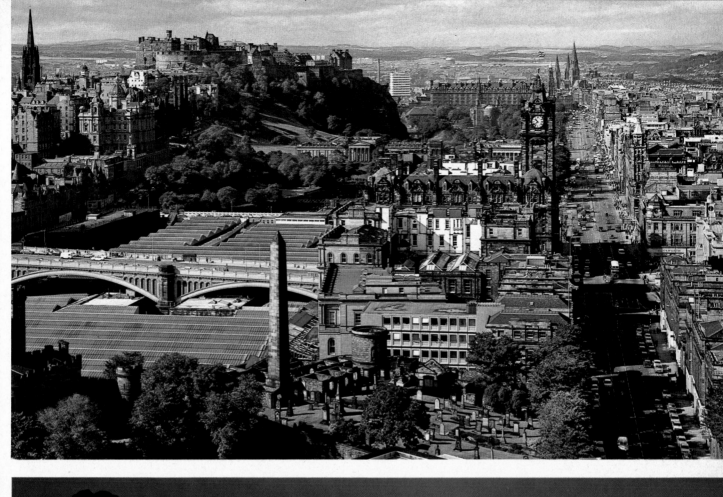

**The Edinburgh Military Tattoo,
Edinburgh Castle** *(Left and Below)*
The Military Tattoo evolved from displays of military drill
during the 1948 Edinburgh International Festival and has
since become a very popular item on the programme. Although
several units from overseas have taken part, the programme is
mainly filled by British bands and display units. There are 27
performances during the three week Festival period, attended
by many thousands of visitors from all over the world.

Forth Bridges, Midlothian *(Below)*
The setting sun reflected in the water throws these two famous bridges into relief with the graded tones of an oriental painting. Both the railway bridge, built in 1883-90, and the recent road suspension bridge beyond are staggering feats of engineering, spanning distances between 2,000 and 3,000 yards, as well as being complementary to the landscape.

The Forth Bridges from the air, Firth of Forth
(Top Right)
Two spectacular bridges span the Firth of Forth from West Lothian to Fife. The rail bridge, a magnificent feat of engineering, was built by Sir John Fowler. It is 2,765 yds. long and the two main spans are each 1,710 ft. The modern road bridge, completed in 1964, is the largest suspension bridge in Europe, being 2,000 yds. long with a centre span of 3,300 ft.

The Forth Bridges from South Queensferry, West Lothian *(Bottom Right)*

St. Andrews Golf Course, Fife *(Top and Bottom Left)*
The Royal and Ancient Golf Club of St. Andrews was founded in 1754 and today is the foremost in the world. Golf is believed to have been played here in the Fifteenth Century. Our picture shows the famous Road Hole, the Seventeenth, on the Old Course.

The Cathedral Ruins, St. Andrews, Fife *(Below)*
Built staunchly facing the cold North Sea, St. Andrews seems braced for more than just the elements. Such inflammatory matters as golf rules, John Knox's sermons and modern students' polemics are in the tradition of the town. The cathedral was founded in 1160 and is just one of the many fascinating places to visit here.

The Harbour, Crail, Fife (Top Left)
Crail, a very old and picturesque fishing town in the east Neuk of Fife, has many buildings dating from the Sixteenth Century. The Church, partly Thirteenth Century, is of considerable interest, as are some of the ancient carved memorials in the churchyard. Of particular charm are the old crow-stepped, and red tiled houses near the harbour.

Anstruther, Fife (Bottom Left)
The harbour, an important fishing port, separates Anstruther Wester from Anstruther Easter, each a Royal Burgh in its own right. Local buildings of historic interest include the Manse, a minister's house dating from 1590 and still occupied, and 16th Century unsupported Church towers which are to be found in both Burghs.

Pittenweem Harbour, Fife (Above)
Old houses frame the busy harbour of Pittenweem, which has been a Royal Burgh since the days of David I. This is a part of Fife once notorious for witches and as late as 1746 a woman was sentenced as a practiser of unholy arts. The imposing church tower, which resembles that of a castle, dates from 1592.

The River Tay from Kinnoull Hill, Perthshire *(Below)*
Kinnoull Hill, east of Perth, rises to a height of 729 ft. and is a magnificent vantage point, affording fine views of the River Tay and the 'Fair City' as well as the beautiful surrounding countryside. From here the river flows between the fertile lands of the Carse of Gowrie and the hills of Fife to the North Sea.

The River Tay, Perth *(Top and Bottom Right)*
Perth, 'The Fair City', stands on the River Tay, which is here spanned by two elegant bridges. Often called 'The Gateway to the Highlands', Perth is an important tourist centre, giving access to much of Scotland's finest scenery. Once the capital of Scotland, the city has many interesting historical connections.

Falls of Dochart, Killin, Perthshire (Below)
The picturesque River Dochart rushes down through the beautiful, deep Glen of the same name to join Loch Tay at Killin. To the north-east stately Ben Lawers, the highest mountain in Perthshire (3,984 ft.), dominates the horizon and provides good ski-ing for visitors to the popular little resort of Killin.

Falls of Orchy, Glen Orchy, Perthshire (Top Right)
The picturesque Falls of Orchy on the river of the same name are a well known beauty spot. Glen Orchy stretches from the Bridge of Orchy where the old and new roads to Glencoe converge, down to Dalmally in the South. Here the river flows into the long expanse of Loch Awe.

Ben Lawers and Loch Tay, Perthshire (Bottom Right)
Ben Lawers overlooks the large and deep Loch Tay, noted for its salmon fishing. The mountain is the highest in Perthshire and of particular botanical interest. The view from its summit, 3,984 ft., is magnificent, taking in the whole of the Breadalbane country and also the Grampians. The slopes of Ben Lawers and surrounding mountains provide good ski-ing and nearby Coire Odhar is used by the Scottish Ski Club.

The Tay Road Bridge *(Top Left)*

The new Tay road Bridge now links Dundee, Angus to Newport-on-Tay, Fife across the Firth of Tay. For many years the crossing had to be made either by rail over the famous two-mile long bridge completed in 1888 or by ferry. The previous tay Rail Bridge was blown down in a great storm in 1879.

Glamis Castle, Angus *(Right)*

Glamis Castle stands in fine grounds bordered by the Dean Water. It is one of the most notable buildings of its period in Scotland and is reputed to be ghost-haunted. The greater part of the structure dates from 1675-1687 but an older tower with 15 ft. thick walls has survived. The great sundial in the foreground is just over 21 ft. in height and has no less than 84 dials.

Dundee by Night *(Bottom Left)*

A striking panorama-by-night of the beautifully situated city and royal burgh of Dundee. Seen from Newport-on-Tay, it includes an excellent view of the Tay Road Bridge. Linking Fife with Dundee and the north, the bridge is a wonderful feat of modern engineering, completed in 1966.

Dundee and the Firth of Tay
with Fife across the River *(Below)*

Dundee, essentially a modern city with extensive docks along the Firth of Tay, has important engineering and shipbuilding industries. At Dundee the river Tay is bridged in two places. The famous rail bridge, dating from 1883, carries the main line from Edinburgh to Aberdeen and the new road bridge, completed in 1966, replaces the old car ferry to Newport-on-Tay.

Loch Tulla, Argyllshire *(Top Left)*
Bordered by the old road to Glencoe, the shores of Loch Tulla are noted for the relics of the pines of the Caledonian Forest. To the north, rise the bleak, undulating moors of Black Mount and the famous peak of Stob Ghabhar, 3,565 ft. To the south, is the attractive old Bridge of Orchy at the entrance to Glen Orchy.

Castle Stalker, Appin, Argyllshire *(Below)*
Standing on a tiny islet in Loch Laich, off Loch Linnhe, Castle Stalker looks on to a region familiar to readers of Robert Louis Stevenson's Kidnapped. Following the rebellion of 1745, the estates of the Stewarts of Appin were forfeited and put under the management of Colin Campbell of Glenure, whose assassination forms part of the plot of the story.

Winter in Ardgour, Argyllshire *(Bottom Left)*
The village of Ardgour is situated on the western shores of Loch Linnhe. Garbh Bheinn, 2,903 ft., is famous among climbers and can be reached on foot by way of the wild Coire an Iubhair. The highest point is the 2,915 ft. high Sgurr Dhomhail which dominates the picturesque Glen Gour.

Tarbert on Loch Fyne, Argyllshire *(Top Left)*
Sheltered in a narrow inlet off Loch Fyne, Tarbert is a happy holiday resort as well as a busy fishing port. Across the hill behind the harbour lies West Tarbert, a gateway to the islands of the Inner Hebrides.

Mull, Argyllshire *(Below)*
Part of the Inner Hebrides, the Isle of Mull guards the entrance to Loch Linnhe and is separated from the mainland by the Sound of Mull to the north and the Firth of Lorne to the south. The undulating scenery of the island is notably picturesque, particularly the rocky coastline with its many sea lochs and tiny bays and inlets. The largest town on the island is Tobermory — famed for the treasure of a Spanish galleon believed to be sunk in the Bay.

The Harbour, Oban, Argyllshire *(Bottom Left)*
Oban is finely situated on the shores of a picturesque bay landlocked by the island of Kerrera. This is a bracing summer resort, the sheltered bay giving beautiful views of sunset amid the mountains of Mull. The immense, circular stone structure known as McCaig's Folly is a vantage point for impressive views of the town and surrounding countryside.

Urquhart Castle and Loch Ness, Inverness-shire *(Top Left)*
On a rocky headland stretching out into the blue waters of
Loch Ness stands the picturesque ruin of Urquhart Castle.
Originally built in the 12th Century, this grim fortress was
sabotaged in 1692 to prevent its capture by the Jacobites.
Loch Ness of 'monster' fame is $22\frac{1}{2}$ miles long and 754 ft. deep.

Aviemore, Inverness-shire *(Below)*
Nestling in the richly wooded Strath Spey which divides the
Cairngorm and Monadhliath mountains, Aviemore is a popular
Highland winter sports resort also offering fine climbing and
walking. To the east is the beautiful 12,500 acre Glen More
National Forest Park with Glenmore Lodge, a mountaineering
training centre.

The Castle, Inverness *(Bottom Left)*
Inverness Castle stands on Castle Hill affording a magnificent
view of the surrounding Highland scenery. It was built on the
site of the former stronghold, destroyed by Bonnie Prince
Charlie during the '45 rebellion. Nearby is a monument to
Flora Macdonald, the Jacobite heroine who helped the Prince
to escape after his defeat at Culloden.

Kyleakin, Isle of Sky, Inverness-shire *(Above)*
Legend has it that the princess who built Castle Moil stretched a chain across the strait — or kyle — of Akin, in order to extract a toll from ships that passed. The magic scenery of Skye, the Misty Island, tempts one to believe such tales without question.

Cuillin Hills, Skye
(Bottom Right)

Loch Laggan, Inverness-shire *(Above)*
Lying between the Monadhliath and Grampian mountains,
Loch Laggan now forms part of the Lochaber Power Scheme.
This area is beautifully wooded and offers some fine scenery,
particularly of the surrounding mountain peaks. To the north
rises Creag Meagaidh, 3,700 ft., reached by way of the wild
Coire Ardair.

**Ben Nevis from the Caledonian Canal,
Inverness-shire** *(Below)*
Winter brings an arctic hue to the Caledonian Canal which follows
the route of the Great Glen and is seen here under the shadow of
Britain's highest mountain, Ben Nevis. Opened in 1822, the
canal's total length is but 4 miles more than a straight line extend-
ing from its eastern to its western extremities.

Dunnottar Castle, Kincardineshire *(Top Left)*
The famous Dunnottar Castle stands on a rocky headland south of Stonehaven. The tower and chapel date from the Fourteenth Century and the gatehouse from the Sixteenth Century. During the Commonwealth Wars, the Scottish regalia were hidden at Dunnottar for safety, but later removed to Kinneff Church.

The Old Bridge of Dee, near Braemar *(Below)*
The splendour of snow-clad Lochnagar makes an impressive backcloth for the Old Bridge of Dee at Invercauld. Set in Royal property, the old bridge dates from 1752 and from here the river flows through Royal Deeside to the sea at Aberdeen.

The Harbour, Gourdon, Kincardineshire *(Bottom Left)*
The fishing vessels are moored and the nets are left drying in the picturesque harbour of Gourdon. The coast line along this part of Kincardine is extremely rocky but the harbour and village of Gourdon are sheltered by Doolie Ness.

Union Street, Aberdeen *(Below)*
The broad, modern thoroughfare of Union Street runs through the heart of Aberdeen. It is flanked by many famous buildings, among them the Town House with its 200 ft. tower and the Church of St. Nicholas. The latter was divided during the Reformation into the East and West Churches and later rebuilt.

Aberdeen *(Top Right)*
The charters of this important city date back to 1179. Today it represents a remarkably clean and solid picture being built largely of granite and often referred to as 'The Granite City'. A popular seaside resort and busy seaport, Aberdeen now plays an increasingly important part in the servicing of the North Sea oil rigs.

The Harbour, Aberdeen *(Bottom Right)*
This famous old city, and Royal Burgh, stands on the estuaries of the Dee and the Don. It is often referred to as the "Granite City", being almost entirely constructed of this stone. It is an important port and hub of the fishing industry, besides having a University, a Cathedral and many other buildings of historic interest.

Macduff, Banffshire *(Below)*
Macduff, opposite the town of Banff on Banff Bay, is an important fishing town with a large harbour to accommodate the fleet of fishing vessels which put out to sea each day. Overlooking the town stands the Hill of Down, a fine viewpoint, bearing a tall war memorial.

Crovie, Banffshire *(Top Right)*
Tucked in the lee of the red cliffs of Gamrie Bay is the secluded fishing village of Crovie. Gamrie Bay has given shelter from enemies as well as the weather and St. John's church on the western arm of the bay was founded in 1004 to commemorate a Scottish victory over the marauding Danes.

Valley of the Avon, Tomintoul, Banff *(Bottom Right)*
To the east of the flat-topped Cairngorms lies the beautiful Valley of the Avon where winter sports alternate with angling to make it an all-year resort. Tomintoul, at 1,160 ft., is the highest village in the Highlands and to the north are the spectacular gorges of Glenlivet and the no-less notable whisky of the Glenlivet distillery.

Eilean Donan Castle, Ross and Cromarty *(Top Right)*
Eilean Donan Castle, the former Macrae stronghold, stands at
the confluence of three lochs, Duich, Long and Alsh. Once
completely surrounded by water, it is linked now by a causeway
to the land. In 1719 the castle was held by a party of Spaniards
in support of a Jacobite Rising and came under fire from the
British frigate, 'Worcester'

Plockton, Ross and Cromarty *(Above)*
Plockton is essentially a fishing and crofting village beautifully
situated on a small inlet of Loch Carron. The county of Ross
and Cromarty stretches across the country from the North Sea
to the Atlantic Ocean and contains every feature of scenic
grandeur peculiar to the Scottish Highlands.

Loch Gairloch, Ross and Cromarty *(Bottom Right)*
Loch Gairloch lies on the west coast of Ross and Cromarty, its
entrance guarded by the small island of Longa. The village of
Gairloch is one of the loveliest in the Highlands, surrounded
by wonderful scenery, and offering excellent bathing and
fishing from its sheltered position on the eastern shore of the
Loch.

Duncansby Head, Caithness *(Top Right)*
This beautiful headland, two miles east of John O' Groats, is a striking viewpoint. Just off the coast, to the south, rise the Stacks of Duncansby, three immense pillars of rock, detached from the mainland by constant sea erosion. Away to the north lie the Orkney Isles.

Badcall, Sutherland *(Above)*
The tiny, remote village of Badcall lies below Laxford Bridge where the noted salmon river, Laxford, enters Loch Laxford. A few small fishing vessels ply the island-studded Loch and the scene is dominated to the south-east by the barren, grey slopes of Ben Stack.

Dunbeath Castle, Caithness *(Bottom Right)*
Perched on the edge of the Caithness plateau, Dunbeath Castle looks deceptively prim with its 19th century facade but it preserves a 15th century keep and was worth capturing by Montrose in 1650. In the hills west of the fishing village of Dunbeath is a granite cross marking the place where tragically, the Duke of Kent's plane crashed in 1942.

Lerwick, Shetland *(Above)*
Capital of the Shetland Islands, Lerwick is the most northerly town in Britain and a busy fishing port. Nearby, King Haco of Norway anchored while en route for the Battle of Largs in 1263. Every January, Lerwick celebrates the Norse festival of Up Helly 'A', a spectacular torchlight procession culminating in the burning of a Viking galley.

Kylesku Ferry, Sutherland *(Bottom Right)*
The vast fjord-like landscapes of the Scottish north-west coast make the scant signs of human activity seem insignificant. Among the many wild and roadless mountains, the Kylesku Ferry, looking like an insect ploughing through the water, bridges the great gap formed by the sea loch Cairnbawn and the inland lochs Glendu and Glencoul.

WALES

Tintern Abbey, Monmouthshire *(Below)*
The ruins of this 12th to 14th century Cistercian Abbey at Tintern
stand in a romantic wooded setting by a curve of the River Wye.
The Wye valley, beginning in the lonely foothills of the mountain
Plynlimon and ending in the Severn estuary, is considered one
of the loveliest valleys in the world.

y Hall, Cardiff *(Above)*
bital of Wales and an important port on the Bristol Channel,
ardiff is also a University City. The castle dates from Norman
mes and was once the home of the Bute family. City Hall is a
magnificent building with a fine 200 ft. clock tower.

Caerphilly Castle, Glamorganshire *(Top Right)*
The town of Caerphilly which lies at the foot of the Rhymney Valley, is well-known for harps and its Caerphilly cheese. Famous too, is the restored castle, the largest in Wales. Dating from the Thirteenth Century, it is the centre-piece of the town.

The Mumbles Lighthouse, Gower, Glamorganshire
(Above)
The Mumbles Lighthouse, on the east coast of the Gower Peninsula, stands on Mumbles Head, guarding the entrance to Swansea Bay. Gower itself is renowned for its wonderful and varied coastal scenery and magnificent beaches. Part of the west coast is a national nature reserve. The village of Mumbles is developing as a resort and has some interesting remains of a Twelfth Century castle.

Barry, Glamorganshire *(Bottom Right)*
Barry is one of the main seaside resorts for the concentrated population of the south of Wales. The wide sandy beaches of Barry Island, the roller-coasters and pony carts near an area of bustling docks are an aspect of Wales that contrasts sharply with the mining districts or the quiet forest regions.

Cit
Car
C
ti

Neuadd Reservoir, Brecon Beacons, Breconshire
(Top Right)

A countryside of colourful mountain and rolling moorland centred around the three distinctive peaks of the 'Beacons' rising to nearly 3,000 feet. The Beacons dominate the whole county as a north-facing scarp of great majesty.

Brecon Beacons National Park, Brecon *(Above)*

The snow-covered peak of Pen-y-Fan, rising to 2,906 ft., is one of the two main summits in the mountain region of Brecon Beacons. This area is largely moorland but to the south the view is enhanced by the crystal clear waters of the Neuadd Reservoirs.

Neuadd Reservoir in Winter, Brecon Beacons National Park *(Bottom Right)*

This magnificent National Park extends from the valley of the River Towy in the west, to the Black Mountains in the east, and includes some of the most beautiful Welsh mountain scenery. Dominating the scene are the peaks of the Beacons themselves, 2,863 ft. and 2,907 ft. from which many small attractive streams flow down to swell the Neuadd and other large reservoirs below.

Pembrokeshire Coast *(Below)*
The wonderful Pembrokeshire Coast stretching from Carmarthen Bay to Cardigan Bay provides some of the most magnificent cliff scenery in Wales. A path winds its way along the cliff tops, providing superb views of the land, sea and in particular the striking rock formations.

Westdale Bay, Dale, Pembrokeshire *(Top Right)*
The charming holiday resort of Dale is situated on a peninsula at the west end of the Haven, where a lighthouse marks the entrance to the estuary. The journey by road round the Westdale Bay is most attractive and, for those on foot, rewarding.

Pembroke Castle, Pembrokeshire *(Bottom Right)*
The original town of Pembroke was situated on an arm of Milford Haven and was separated from the imposing Norman Castle by a ditch. The castle walls formerly encircled the town of Pembroke and the remaining parts give the town a picturesque appearance.

Lydstep, Pembrokeshire *(Top Left)*
The view from the cliffs at Lydstep gives a good impression of
the ruggedness of this part of the coast. The deep descent to
Lydstep Caves can be made by foot only at low tides but the
journey can also be made by boat when the view of these rocky
mounds is awe-inspiring.

St. David's Cathedral, Pembrokeshire *(Bottom Left)*
The straggling village of St. David's is dominated by its
Cathedral. Traditionally St. David, patron saint of Wales, is said
to have founded a church and monastery on this site. On the
north side of the Cathedral Nave are the ruins of St. Mary's
College, once connected to the Cathedral by a cloister.

Fishguard, Pembrokeshire *(Above)*
Fishguard is a picturesque little fishing village perched high
above the old harbour. This small port and bay is also a holiday resort having fine cliff views and bathing from a shingly
beach. It was near here that the French made an unsuccessful
attempt to land in 1797.

Tresaith, Cardiganshire *(Top Left)*
A very attractive little cliff-top village, Tresaith, or Traeth Saith, lies some miles south-west of New Quay on Cardigan Bay. The sheltered beach is flanked by rugged cliffs and is a favourite haunt of holiday-makers. To the south lies Aberporth and to the north Llangranog, both pretty villages with lovely sands and bathing.

Aberystwyth, Cardiganshire *(Bottom Left)*
A popular holiday resort, Aberystwyth lies on Cardigan Bay and it was here that the first College of the University of Wales was opened in 1872. Of interest are the ruined Norman Castle and the National Library of Wales. The town gives access to the beautiful Valley of Rheidol, affording exceptionally lovely scenery.

Furnace Falls, Cardiganshire *(Above)*
Autumn tints set off the splendour of the Furnace Falls — one of the many picturesque scenes that this country has to offer. In complete contrast are the desolate sea marshes of Cors Fochno which lie between Furnace and the Dyfi estuary.

Tal-y-llyn, Merionethshire *(Top Left)*
An unusual way of visiting Tal-y-llyn in the summer months is by the Tal-y-llyn Railway. This railway still uses its original rolling stock from 1865 and is the oldest steam-hauled narrow gauge passenger railway in the world. In these days of rush and hurry this is a most relaxing and picturesque journey.

Harlech Castle, Merionethshire *(Bottom Left)*
The name Harlech rings through history as the last stronghold of the Lancastrians in North Wales and the last held by the Royalists in the Civil War. In the setting sun, the redoubtable gateway and silhouetted towers regain their war-like appearance as perhaps they looked when Edward I completed them in the 13th century.

Dolgoch, nr. Towyn, Merionethshire *(Above)*
The leafy branches and wet green bracken frame a classic scene of a shepherd driving his sheep with only his dogs for company. Deep in the Cader Idris mountains, Dolgoch is renowned for its beautiful waterfalls and the region offers quiet valleys and rocky precipices for the rambler.

Caernarvon Castle *(Left and Below)*
It was in this famous Thirteenth Century castle, now restored, that the first Prince of Wales, later Edward II, was born and presented to the people in 1284. The town lies on the Menai Strait and the walls, also Thirteenth Century, are well preserved. The church has a Tudor tower and parts date from the Fourteenth and Sixteenth Centuries.

Aberglaslyn, Caernarvonshire (Left)

The wooded valley of Aberglaslyn is surrounded by magnificent scenery and dominated by the 2,860 ft. Moel Siabod to the east. Many attractive little rivers and streams provide excellent fishing, and the picturesque Snowdon and Ffestiniog Railways are great attractions to visitors, as are the surrounding awe-inspiring mountains.

Conway, Caernarvonshire (Top Right)

Conway, on the estuary of the River Conway, is an attractive resort with a picturesque old quay for fishing vessels and good beaches. Much of the old town walls remain and the Thirteenth Century castle, now in ruins, is also of interest. Here too, is Telford's fine road bridge, now owned by the National Trust.

Llandudno from Great Orme, Caernarvonshire
(Bottom Right)

The famous Great Ormes Head, 679 ft., overlooks the beautiful blue sweep of Llandudno Bay with its fine beach and good bathing. The Head is encircled by Marine Drive, a toll road providing splendid views of the sea. The headland can also be ascended by a cable tramway. The summit affords striking views of the coast and further inland the undulating mountains.

The Snowdon Mountain Railway, Caernarvonshire
(Below)

The famous rack railway runs from Llanberis during the summer months up the steep, barren mountainside to the summit of the 3,560 ft. Snowdon, the highest mountain in England and Wales. For those who brave the journey past the waterfall and through Hebron station above the sheer Clogwyn Du'r Arddu, the views are no small reward.

The Menai Suspension Bridge, Anglesey *(Top Left)*

Telford's magnificent suspension bridge took five and a half years to complete and was opened in 1826. Originally constructed to carry stage-coach traffic, the bridge was reinforced and widened between 1938 and 1941 to cope with heavy motor vehicles. The distance between the two piers is 580 ft. and the total length of the bridge 1,265 ft. Today, it still dominates the scene, carrying many hundreds of visitors to Anglesey.

Benllech Bay, Anglesey *(Bottom Left)*

The tiny village of Benllech lies on the east coast of Anglesey to the north of Red Wharf Bay. There is a fine, sandy beach with safe bathing. The nearby countryside is of great interest to geologists and many fossils have been found in the area.

South Stack Lighthouse, Anglesey *(Above)*

Dramatically situated off the west coast of Anglesey and connected to the mainland by an early suspension bridge, South Stack Lighthouse presents an awe-inspiring picture. It was built in 1809 and, when foggy weather obscured the tower, a small light was lowered to within 60 ft. of the water to warn shipping. The station is now unmanned.

Plas Newydd, Llangollen, Denbighshire *(Below)*
This beautiful and famous Eighteenth Century mansion was the
home of the Honourable Sarah Ponsonby and Lady Eleanor
Butler, affectionately known as the 'Ladies of Llangollen'.
Standing on the lovely River Dee, the town of Llangollen is
surrounded by wonderful countryside in the Vale of Llangollen.
A Fourteenth Century bridge spans the Dee here, traditionally
known as one of the Seven Wonders of Wales.

NORTHERN IRELAND

Queen's University, Belfast *(Above)*
South of the centre of Belfast in University Street stands the
wonderful old Tudor style building of Queen's University with
its square tower. Founded in 1849, it became a separate
University in 1908 and now incorporates excellent, up-to-date
teaching facilities.

Lough Neagh, Co. Antrim *(Top Right)*
Lough Neagh is the largest stretch of inland water in Great Britain. Sheltered at the eastern end by the hills of Belfast, it lies in picturesque surroundings and is traditionally said to have been formed by the overflowing of a fountain. Coney Island which lies at the south-west extremity of the Lough has associations with St. Patrick.

Coast near Portrush, Co. Antrim *(Above)*
The fine beaches near Portrush are intriguing with their beautiful caves and strange rock formations. Looking out to the Atlantic, Portrush, on its basalt peninsula, is a favourite resort with its dramatic views of the Donegal mountains to one side and the many islands on the other. On a clear day the Mull of Kintyre in Scotland can be seen.

Kenbane Castle, Antrim *(Bottom Right)*
Kenbane Castle stands some $3\frac{1}{2}$ miles north-west of Ballycastle. It was built by Colla McDonnell in 1547, attacked by the English and finally captured and sacked in 1551 by Sir Thomas Cusack. Later it was restored and re-occupied by Colla and, on his death in 1558, passed to his younger brother, the renowned Sorley Boye McDonnell of nearby Dunanynie. It is now in the charge of the Antrim County Council.

Ballintoy Harbour, Co. Antrim *(Below)*
The pretty harbour of Ballintoy village looks out to Rathlin Island, the stocking-shaped island and stepping stone to Scotland. A grassy path leads off to the west to Whitepark Bay, paradise for naturalists and archaelogical enthusiasts. To the east is Carrickarade Island, linked to the mainland by a fearsome rope bridge.

Carrickfergus Castle, Co. Antrim *(Top Right)*
Carrickfergus is a few miles south of Larne, terminal of the shortest sea route from Britain. The Castle, built by the Normans, has been restored to keep its original 13th century character. Within its ramparts King John, Edward Bruce, Con o'Neil of Clandeboye and many others have played their part in history and legend.

Bushmills, Co. Antrim *(Bottom Right)*
The village of Bushmills is situated on the river Bush which provides excellent fishing. it is not far inland from the pleasant beach of Portballintrae. However the mills, the nine-hole golf course and the fishing all pale in comparison with the quality of the whiskey they make in the Bushmills distillery.

Ballycopeland Windmill, Millisle, Co. Down *(Right)*

Situated on the low-lying Ards Peninsula, the famous Bally-copeland Windmill is one of the few mills in existence in Ireland. It is believed to date from the 16th century and has wooden parts, still in working order. Nearby Carrowdore Castle was the home of the Huguenot family who introduced the linen industry to Ireland.

Dundrum and the Mountains of Mourne, Co. Down
(Top Left)

The village of Dundrum stands on the shores of Dundrum Bay. An attractive little fishing port, it has the ruin of an historic castle. The keep is circular and is a magnificent vantage point from which to view the beautiful surrounding scenery and the Mourne Mountains which lie some few miles to the south-west.

Kilkeel Harbour, Co. Down *(Bottom Left)*

Kilkeel, the Church of the Narrow, is an attractive and prosperous resort with a beautiful beach and busy fishing and yachting harbour. At one time it was the capital of the erstwhile Kingdom of Mourne and affords excellent views of the magnificent lofty mountains with their fine scenery and silent loughs.

Ardglass, Co. Down *(Below)*

A famous port in the Middle Ages, Ardglass is now a centre of the herring fishing industry. Colonised by the English at the time of Henry IV, the town was surrounded by a ring of castles many of which, although now in ruins, can still be seen. Jordan's Castle is well preserved and is open to the public.

Portstewart Strand, Co. Derry *(Above)*

The curving arm of the rocky outcrop that supports the town forms a shelter for the beach of Portstewart Strand. The town is proud possessor of two eighteen-hole golf courses. Although the temperature is not always suitable for swimming, the white beach and blue waters always invite one to pause and admire.

The Guildhall, Londonderry *(Right)*

Londonderry derives its name from the granting of the city to a body of London merchants. It was previously known as Derry-Columbkille after St. Columba who founded a monastery on the site in 546. The Guildhall, rebuilt in 1908, the previous building having been destroyed by fire, has a fine bell tower and several interesting stained glass windows presented by the London Companies.

Kesh Bay, Lough Erne, Co. Fermanagh *(Below Left)*

The magic of Ireland is ever present as dusk falls on Kesh Bay. Nearby the stone circles of a Bronze Age temple stand as they have for centuries. Though Kesh boasts of a sailing school and three ski clubs, these do not ruffle the waters of the lake as often as the ducks and fish which abound among the islands.

Barnes Gap, Co. Tyrone *(Above)*

Barnes Gap, famed for its lovely scenery, is a three-mile cleft through the mountains between the winding Glenelly and Owenkillew river valleys. Though peaceful now, this was the land of highwaymen and kidnappers and in the Sperrin mountains on the far side of the Glenelly, the last wolf in Ireland was shot two centuries ago.

Monea Castle, Co. Fermanagh *(Right)*

To the south of Lough Erne, in the heart of the Irish lake district, stands Monea Castle which is named Ma Nia — the Plain of Heroes. The castle is a splendid example of the fortified homes built by the Scottish ar.d English settlers and the well-preserved structure features the crow-stepped gables reminiscent of Scotland.

The Mountains of Mourne, Co. Down *(Above)*
The famous Mourne Mountains, rendered immortal in song
and verse, are the highest in Northern Ireland. Dominated by
Slieve Donard, 2,796 ft., which rises to the south-west of
Newcastle, the tallest peaks command a fine view, on a clear
day, across the Irish Sea to the Isles of Arran and Man.

White Rocks, Portrush, Co. Antrim *(Below)*
The name Portrush is derived from the Gaelic 'Port Rois' meaning Harbour of the Headland and the town is indeed situated on the rocky Ramore Head jutting almost a mile out into the sea. The peninsula is believed to have been the site of an English fort as it was at one time sold to an English adventurer for 'a hogshead of claret yearly'.